This Paranormal Investigation Notebook Belongs To

_____

If Found Please Contact

_____

Investigation Index

26 _____

27 _____

28 _____

29 _____

30 _____

31 _____

32 _____

33 _____

34 _____

35 _____

36 _____

37 _____

38 _____

39 _____

40 _____

41 _____

42 _____

43 _____

44 _____

45 _____

46 _____

47 _____

48 _____

49 _____

50 _____

🔍 CASE NUMBER	
📅 DATE	
🕐 START / END TIME	
📍 LOCATION	
📇 ADDRESS	
👥 CLIENT	
👥 PARTICIPANTS	

SITE INFORMATION

✦ KNOWN HAUNTING	🚪 ROOM/ LOCATION	📄 DESCRIPTION

SUSPECTED ENTITY INFORMATION

POSSIBLE NAMES	
DATES ALIVE	
KNOWN MOTIVE & STORY	

INVESTIGATION RECORDINGS

TEMPERATURE		SENSOR READING 1	
ATMOSPHERE		SENSOR READING 2	

OBSERVATIONS

EQUIPMENT/ INVESTIGATOR	REPORTS & NOTES

PHOTOS/ SKETCHES

CASE NUMBER

DATE

START / END TIME

LOCATION

ADDRESS

CLIENT

PARTICIPANTS

SITE INFORMATION

✧ KNOWN HAUNTING	▯ ROOM/ LOCATION	🗎 DESCRIPTION

SUSPECTED ENTITY INFORMATION

POSSIBLE NAMES	
DATES ALIVE	
KNOWN MOTIVE & STORY	

INVESTIGATION RECORDINGS

TEMPERATURE		SENSOR READING 1	
ATMOSPHERE		SENSOR READING 2	

OBSERVATIONS

EQUIPMENT/ INVESTIGATOR	REPORTS & NOTES

PHOTOS/ SKETCHES

🔍 CASE NUMBER
📅 DATE
⏱ START / END TIME
📍 LOCATION
📇 ADDRESS
👥 CLIENT
👥 PARTICIPANTS

SITE INFORMATION

✨ KNOWN HAUNTING	🚪 ROOM/ LOCATION	📄 DESCRIPTION

SUSPECTED ENTITY INFORMATION

POSSIBLE NAMES	
DATES ALIVE	
KNOWN MOTIVE & STORY	

INVESTIGATION RECORDINGS

TEMPERATURE		SENSOR READING 1	
ATMOSPHERE		SENSOR READING 2	

OBSERVATIONS

EQUIPMENT/ INVESTIGATOR	REPORTS & NOTES

PHOTOS/ SKETCHES

🔍 CASE NUMBER
📅 DATE
🕐 START / END TIME
📍 LOCATION
📇 ADDRESS
👥 CLIENT
👥 PARTICIPANTS

SITE INFORMATION

✨ KNOWN HAUNTING	🚪 ROOM/ LOCATION	📄 DESCRIPTION

SUSPECTED ENTITY INFORMATION

POSSIBLE NAMES	
DATES ALIVE	
KNOWN MOTIVE & STORY	

INVESTIGATION RECORDINGS

TEMPERATURE		SENSOR READING 1	
ATMOSPHERE		SENSOR READING 2	

OBSERVATIONS

⊚ EQUIPMENT/ INVESTIGATOR	📝 REPORTS & NOTES

PHOTOS/ SKETCHES

🔍 CASE NUMBER
📅 DATE
🕐 START / END TIME
📍 LOCATION
📇 ADDRESS
👥 CLIENT
👥 PARTICIPANTS

SITE INFORMATION

✨ KNOWN HAUNTING	🚪 ROOM/ LOCATION	📄 DESCRIPTION

SUSPECTED ENTITY INFORMATION

POSSIBLE NAMES	
DATES ALIVE	
KNOWN MOTIVE & STORY	

INVESTIGATION RECORDINGS

TEMPERATURE		SENSOR READING 1	
ATMOSPHERE		SENSOR READING 2	

OBSERVATIONS

EQUIPMENT/ INVESTIGATOR	REPORTS & NOTES

PHOTOS/ SKETCHES

🔍 CASE NUMBER	
📅 DATE	
⏱ START / END TIME	
📍 LOCATION	
📇 ADDRESS	
👥 CLIENT	
👥 PARTICIPANTS	

SITE INFORMATION

✨ KNOWN HAUNTING	🚪 ROOM/ LOCATION	📄 DESCRIPTION

SUSPECTED ENTITY INFORMATION

POSSIBLE NAMES	
DATES ALIVE	
KNOWN MOTIVE & STORY	

INVESTIGATION RECORDINGS

TEMPERATURE		SENSOR READING 1	
ATMOSPHERE		SENSOR READING 2	

OBSERVATIONS

EQUIPMENT/ INVESTIGATOR	REPORTS & NOTES

PHOTOS/ SKETCHES

🔍 CASE NUMBER
📅 DATE
🕙 START / END TIME
📍 LOCATION
📇 ADDRESS
👥 CLIENT
👥 PARTICIPANTS

SITE INFORMATION

✦ KNOWN HAUNTING	🚪 ROOM/ LOCATION	📄 DESCRIPTION

SUSPECTED ENTITY INFORMATION

POSSIBLE NAMES	
DATES ALIVE	
KNOWN MOTIVE & STORY	

INVESTIGATION RECORDINGS

TEMPERATURE		SENSOR READING 1	
ATMOSPHERE		SENSOR READING 2	

OBSERVATIONS

EQUIPMENT/ INVESTIGATOR	REPORTS & NOTES

PHOTOS/ SKETCHES

🔍 CASE NUMBER	
📅 DATE	
🕐 START / END TIME	
📍 LOCATION	
📇 ADDRESS	
👥 CLIENT	
👥 PARTICIPANTS	

SITE INFORMATION

✨ KNOWN HAUNTING	🚪 ROOM/ LOCATION	📄 DESCRIPTION

SUSPECTED ENTITY INFORMATION

POSSIBLE NAMES	
DATES ALIVE	
KNOWN MOTIVE & STORY	

INVESTIGATION RECORDINGS

TEMPERATURE		SENSOR READING 1	
ATMOSPHERE		SENSOR READING 2	

OBSERVATIONS

EQUIPMENT/ INVESTIGATOR	REPORTS & NOTES

PHOTOS/ SKETCHES

🔍 CASE NUMBER
📅 DATE
⏱ START / END TIME
📍 LOCATION
📇 ADDRESS
👥 CLIENT
👥 PARTICIPANTS

SITE INFORMATION

✨ KNOWN HAUNTING	🚪 ROOM/ LOCATION	📄 DESCRIPTION

SUSPECTED ENTITY INFORMATION

POSSIBLE NAMES	
DATES ALIVE	
KNOWN MOTIVE & STORY	

INVESTIGATION RECORDINGS

TEMPERATURE		SENSOR READING 1	
ATMOSPHERE		SENSOR READING 2	

OBSERVATIONS

EQUIPMENT/ INVESTIGATOR	REPORTS & NOTES

PHOTOS/ SKETCHES

🔍 CASE NUMBER
📅 DATE
🕐 START / END TIME
📍 LOCATION
📇 ADDRESS
👥 CLIENT
👥 PARTICIPANTS

SITE INFORMATION

✧ KNOWN HAUNTING	🚪 ROOM/ LOCATION	📄 DESCRIPTION

SUSPECTED ENTITY INFORMATION

POSSIBLE NAMES	
DATES ALIVE	
KNOWN MOTIVE & STORY	

INVESTIGATION RECORDINGS

TEMPERATURE		SENSOR READING 1	
ATMOSPHERE		SENSOR READING 2	

OBSERVATIONS

EQUIPMENT/ INVESTIGATOR	REPORTS & NOTES

PHOTOS/ SKETCHES

🔍 CASE NUMBER	
📅 DATE	
🕐 START / END TIME	
📍 LOCATION	
📖 ADDRESS	
👥 CLIENT	
👥 PARTICIPANTS	

SITE INFORMATION

✧ KNOWN HAUNTING	🚪 ROOM/ LOCATION	📄 DESCRIPTION

SUSPECTED ENTITY INFORMATION

POSSIBLE NAMES	
DATES ALIVE	
KNOWN MOTIVE & STORY	

INVESTIGATION RECORDINGS

TEMPERATURE		SENSOR READING 1	
ATMOSPHERE		SENSOR READING 2	

OBSERVATIONS

EQUIPMENT/ INVESTIGATOR	REPORTS & NOTES

PHOTOS/ SKETCHES

🔍 CASE NUMBER	
🗓️ DATE	
🕐 START / END TIME	
🏠 LOCATION	
📇 ADDRESS	
👥 CLIENT	
👥 PARTICIPANTS	

SITE INFORMATION

✧ KNOWN HAUNTING	🚪 ROOM/ LOCATION	📄 DESCRIPTION

SUSPECTED ENTITY INFORMATION

POSSIBLE NAMES	
DATES ALIVE	
KNOWN MOTIVE & STORY	

INVESTIGATION RECORDINGS

TEMPERATURE		SENSOR READING 1	
ATMOSPHERE		SENSOR READING 2	

OBSERVATIONS

EQUIPMENT/ INVESTIGATOR	REPORTS & NOTES

PHOTOS/ SKETCHES

🔍 CASE NUMBER	
📅 DATE	
🕐 START / END TIME	
📍 LOCATION	
📇 ADDRESS	
👥 CLIENT	
👥 PARTICIPANTS	

SITE INFORMATION

✦ KNOWN HAUNTING	🚪 ROOM/ LOCATION	📄 DESCRIPTION

SUSPECTED ENTITY INFORMATION

POSSIBLE NAMES	
DATES ALIVE	
KNOWN MOTIVE & STORY	

INVESTIGATION RECORDINGS

TEMPERATURE		SENSOR READING 1	
ATMOSPHERE		SENSOR READING 2	

OBSERVATIONS

EQUIPMENT/ INVESTIGATOR	REPORTS & NOTES

PHOTOS/ SKETCHES

CASE NUMBER

DATE

START / END TIME

LOCATION

ADDRESS

CLIENT

PARTICIPANTS

SITE INFORMATION

KNOWN HAUNTING	ROOM/ LOCATION	DESCRIPTION

SUSPECTED ENTITY INFORMATION

POSSIBLE NAMES	
DATES ALIVE	
KNOWN MOTIVE & STORY	

INVESTIGATION RECORDINGS

TEMPERATURE		SENSOR READING 1	
ATMOSPHERE		SENSOR READING 2	

OBSERVATIONS

EQUIPMENT/ INVESTIGATOR	REPORTS & NOTES

PHOTOS/ SKETCHES

🔍 CASE NUMBER
📅 DATE
🕐 START / END TIME
📍 LOCATION
📇 ADDRESS
👥 CLIENT
👥 PARTICIPANTS

SITE INFORMATION

✨ KNOWN HAUNTING	🚪 ROOM/ LOCATION	📄 DESCRIPTION

SUSPECTED ENTITY INFORMATION

POSSIBLE NAMES	
DATES ALIVE	
KNOWN MOTIVE & STORY	

INVESTIGATION RECORDINGS

TEMPERATURE		SENSOR READING 1	
ATMOSPHERE		SENSOR READING 2	

OBSERVATIONS

EQUIPMENT/ INVESTIGATOR	REPORTS & NOTES

PHOTOS/ SKETCHES

🔍 CASE NUMBER	
📅 DATE	
🕐 START / END TIME	
📍 LOCATION	
📇 ADDRESS	
👥 CLIENT	
👥 PARTICIPANTS	

SITE INFORMATION

✦ KNOWN HAUNTING	🚪 ROOM/ LOCATION	📄 DESCRIPTION

SUSPECTED ENTITY INFORMATION

POSSIBLE NAMES	
DATES ALIVE	
KNOWN MOTIVE & STORY	

INVESTIGATION RECORDINGS

TEMPERATURE		SENSOR READING 1	
ATMOSPHERE		SENSOR READING 2	

OBSERVATIONS

EQUIPMENT/ INVESTIGATOR	REPORTS & NOTES

PHOTOS/ SKETCHES

🔍 CASE NUMBER
📅 DATE
🕐 START / END TIME
📍 LOCATION
📇 ADDRESS
👥 CLIENT
👥 PARTICIPANTS

SITE INFORMATION

✧ KNOWN HAUNTING	🚪 ROOM/ LOCATION	📄 DESCRIPTION

SUSPECTED ENTITY INFORMATION

POSSIBLE NAMES	
DATES ALIVE	
KNOWN MOTIVE & STORY	

INVESTIGATION RECORDINGS

TEMPERATURE		SENSOR READING 1	
ATMOSPHERE		SENSOR READING 2	

OBSERVATIONS

EQUIPMENT/ INVESTIGATOR	REPORTS & NOTES

PHOTOS/ SKETCHES

🔍 CASE NUMBER	
📅 DATE	
🕐 START / END TIME	
📍 LOCATION	
📇 ADDRESS	
👥 CLIENT	
👥 PARTICIPANTS	

SITE INFORMATION

✧ KNOWN HAUNTING	🚪 ROOM/ LOCATION	📄 DESCRIPTION

SUSPECTED ENTITY INFORMATION

POSSIBLE NAMES	
DATES ALIVE	
KNOWN MOTIVE & STORY	

INVESTIGATION RECORDINGS

TEMPERATURE		SENSOR READING 1	
ATMOSPHERE		SENSOR READING 2	

OBSERVATIONS

(⊚) EQUIPMENT/ INVESTIGATOR	📝 REPORTS & NOTES

PHOTOS/ SKETCHES

🔍 CASE NUMBER	
🗓️ DATE	
🕐 START / END TIME	
📍 LOCATION	
🏛️ ADDRESS	
👥 CLIENT	
👥 PARTICIPANTS	

SITE INFORMATION

✨ KNOWN HAUNTING	🚪 ROOM/ LOCATION	📄 DESCRIPTION

SUSPECTED ENTITY INFORMATION

POSSIBLE NAMES	
DATES ALIVE	
KNOWN MOTIVE & STORY	

INVESTIGATION RECORDINGS

TEMPERATURE		SENSOR READING 1	
ATMOSPHERE		SENSOR READING 2	

OBSERVATIONS

EQUIPMENT/ INVESTIGATOR	REPORTS & NOTES

PHOTOS/ SKETCHES

🔍 **CASE NUMBER**		
📅 **DATE**		
🕐 **START / END TIME**		
📍 **LOCATION**		
📇 **ADDRESS**		
👥 **CLIENT**		
👥 **PARTICIPANTS**		

SITE INFORMATION

✨ KNOWN HAUNTING	🚪 ROOM/ LOCATION	📄 DESCRIPTION

SUSPECTED ENTITY INFORMATION

POSSIBLE NAMES	
DATES ALIVE	
KNOWN MOTIVE & STORY	

INVESTIGATION RECORDINGS

TEMPERATURE		SENSOR READING 1	
ATMOSPHERE		SENSOR READING 2	

OBSERVATIONS

EQUIPMENT/ INVESTIGATOR	REPORTS & NOTES

PHOTOS/ SKETCHES

🔍 CASE NUMBER
📅 DATE
⏱ START / END TIME
📍 LOCATION
📇 ADDRESS
👥 CLIENT
👥 PARTICIPANTS

SITE INFORMATION

✧ KNOWN HAUNTING	🚪 ROOM/ LOCATION	📄 DESCRIPTION

SUSPECTED ENTITY INFORMATION

POSSIBLE NAMES	
DATES ALIVE	
KNOWN MOTIVE & STORY	

INVESTIGATION RECORDINGS

TEMPERATURE		SENSOR READING 1	
ATMOSPHERE		SENSOR READING 2	

OBSERVATIONS

EQUIPMENT/ INVESTIGATOR	REPORTS & NOTES

PHOTOS/ SKETCHES

🔍 CASE NUMBER	
📅 DATE	
⏱ START / END TIME	
🏠 LOCATION	
📇 ADDRESS	
👥 CLIENT	
👥 PARTICIPANTS	

SITE INFORMATION

✦ KNOWN HAUNTING	🚪 ROOM/ LOCATION	📄 DESCRIPTION

SUSPECTED ENTITY INFORMATION

POSSIBLE NAMES	
DATES ALIVE	
KNOWN MOTIVE & STORY	

INVESTIGATION RECORDINGS

TEMPERATURE		SENSOR READING 1	
ATMOSPHERE		SENSOR READING 2	

OBSERVATIONS

EQUIPMENT/ INVESTIGATOR	REPORTS & NOTES

PHOTOS/ SKETCHES

🔍 CASE NUMBER
📅 DATE
⏱ START / END TIME
📍 LOCATION
📇 ADDRESS
👥 CLIENT
👥 PARTICIPANTS

SITE INFORMATION

✨ KNOWN HAUNTING	🚪 ROOM/ LOCATION	📄 DESCRIPTION

SUSPECTED ENTITY INFORMATION

POSSIBLE NAMES	
DATES ALIVE	
KNOWN MOTIVE & STORY	

INVESTIGATION RECORDINGS

TEMPERATURE		SENSOR READING 1	
ATMOSPHERE		SENSOR READING 2	

OBSERVATIONS

⊘ EQUIPMENT/ INVESTIGATOR	📝 REPORTS & NOTES

PHOTOS/ SKETCHES

🔍 CASE NUMBER	
📅 DATE	
🕐 START / END TIME	
📍 LOCATION	
📇 ADDRESS	
👥 CLIENT	
👥 PARTICIPANTS	

SITE INFORMATION

✨ KNOWN HAUNTING	🚪 ROOM/ LOCATION	📄 DESCRIPTION

SUSPECTED ENTITY INFORMATION

POSSIBLE NAMES	
DATES ALIVE	
KNOWN MOTIVE & STORY	

INVESTIGATION RECORDINGS

TEMPERATURE		SENSOR READING 1	
ATMOSPHERE		SENSOR READING 2	

OBSERVATIONS

EQUIPMENT/ INVESTIGATOR	REPORTS & NOTES

PHOTOS/ SKETCHES

🔍 CASE NUMBER	
📅 DATE	
⏱ START / END TIME	
📍 LOCATION	
📇 ADDRESS	
👥 CLIENT	
👥 PARTICIPANTS	

SITE INFORMATION

✨ KNOWN HAUNTING	🚪 ROOM/ LOCATION	📄 DESCRIPTION

SUSPECTED ENTITY INFORMATION

POSSIBLE NAMES	
DATES ALIVE	
KNOWN MOTIVE & STORY	

INVESTIGATION RECORDINGS

TEMPERATURE		SENSOR READING 1	
ATMOSPHERE		SENSOR READING 2	

OBSERVATIONS

⊙ EQUIPMENT/ INVESTIGATOR	📝 REPORTS & NOTES

PHOTOS/ SKETCHES

🔍 CASE NUMBER	
📅 DATE	
🕐 START / END TIME	
📍 LOCATION	
📇 ADDRESS	
👥 CLIENT	
👥 PARTICIPANTS	

SITE INFORMATION

✨ KNOWN HAUNTING	🚪 ROOM/ LOCATION	📄 DESCRIPTION

SUSPECTED ENTITY INFORMATION

POSSIBLE NAMES	
DATES ALIVE	
KNOWN MOTIVE & STORY	

INVESTIGATION RECORDINGS

TEMPERATURE		SENSOR READING 1	
ATMOSPHERE		SENSOR READING 2	

OBSERVATIONS

EQUIPMENT/ INVESTIGATOR	REPORTS & NOTES

PHOTOS/ SKETCHES

🔍 CASE NUMBER	
📅 DATE	
⏱ START / END TIME	
📍 LOCATION	
📇 ADDRESS	
👥 CLIENT	
👥 PARTICIPANTS	

SITE INFORMATION

✧ KNOWN HAUNTING	🚪 ROOM/ LOCATION	📄 DESCRIPTION

SUSPECTED ENTITY INFORMATION

POSSIBLE NAMES	
DATES ALIVE	
KNOWN MOTIVE & STORY	

INVESTIGATION RECORDINGS

TEMPERATURE		SENSOR READING 1	
ATMOSPHERE		SENSOR READING 2	

OBSERVATIONS

EQUIPMENT/ INVESTIGATOR	REPORTS & NOTES

PHOTOS/ SKETCHES

🔍 CASE NUMBER	
📅 DATE	
🕐 START / END TIME	
📍 LOCATION	
📇 ADDRESS	
👥 CLIENT	
👥 PARTICIPANTS	

SITE INFORMATION

✧ KNOWN HAUNTING	🚪 ROOM/ LOCATION	📄 DESCRIPTION

SUSPECTED ENTITY INFORMATION

POSSIBLE NAMES	
DATES ALIVE	
KNOWN MOTIVE & STORY	

INVESTIGATION RECORDINGS

TEMPERATURE		SENSOR READING 1	
ATMOSPHERE		SENSOR READING 2	

OBSERVATIONS

EQUIPMENT/ INVESTIGATOR	REPORTS & NOTES

PHOTOS/ SKETCHES

🔍 CASE NUMBER
📅 DATE
⏱ START / END TIME
📍 LOCATION
📇 ADDRESS
👥 CLIENT
👥 PARTICIPANTS

SITE INFORMATION

✨ KNOWN HAUNTING	🚪 ROOM/ LOCATION	📄 DESCRIPTION

SUSPECTED ENTITY INFORMATION

POSSIBLE NAMES	
DATES ALIVE	
KNOWN MOTIVE & STORY	

INVESTIGATION RECORDINGS

TEMPERATURE		SENSOR READING 1	
ATMOSPHERE		SENSOR READING 2	

OBSERVATIONS

⊚ EQUIPMENT/ INVESTIGATOR	📝 REPORTS & NOTES

PHOTOS/ SKETCHES

🔍 CASE NUMBER	
📅 DATE	
⏱ START / END TIME	
📍 LOCATION	
📇 ADDRESS	
👥 CLIENT	
👥 PARTICIPANTS	

SITE INFORMATION

✧ KNOWN HAUNTING	🚪 ROOM/ LOCATION	📄 DESCRIPTION

SUSPECTED ENTITY INFORMATION

POSSIBLE NAMES	
DATES ALIVE	
KNOWN MOTIVE & STORY	

INVESTIGATION RECORDINGS

TEMPERATURE		SENSOR READING 1	
ATMOSPHERE		SENSOR READING 2	

OBSERVATIONS

EQUIPMENT/ INVESTIGATOR	REPORTS & NOTES

PHOTOS/ SKETCHES

🔍 CASE NUMBER	
📅 DATE	
🕐 START / END TIME	
📍 LOCATION	
📇 ADDRESS	
👥 CLIENT	
👥 PARTICIPANTS	

SITE INFORMATION

✨ KNOWN HAUNTING	🚪 ROOM/ LOCATION	📄 DESCRIPTION

SUSPECTED ENTITY INFORMATION

POSSIBLE NAMES	
DATES ALIVE	
KNOWN MOTIVE & STORY	

INVESTIGATION RECORDINGS

TEMPERATURE		SENSOR READING 1	
ATMOSPHERE		SENSOR READING 2	

OBSERVATIONS

⊘ EQUIPMENT/ INVESTIGATOR	📝 REPORTS & NOTES

PHOTOS/ SKETCHES

🔍 CASE NUMBER	
📅 DATE	
⏱ START / END TIME	
📍 LOCATION	
📇 ADDRESS	
👥 CLIENT	
👥 PARTICIPANTS	

SITE INFORMATION

✦ KNOWN HAUNTING	🚪 ROOM/ LOCATION	📄 DESCRIPTION

SUSPECTED ENTITY INFORMATION

POSSIBLE NAMES	
DATES ALIVE	
KNOWN MOTIVE & STORY	

INVESTIGATION RECORDINGS

TEMPERATURE		SENSOR READING 1	
ATMOSPHERE		SENSOR READING 2	

OBSERVATIONS

EQUIPMENT/ INVESTIGATOR	REPORTS & NOTES

PHOTOS/ SKETCHES

🔍 CASE NUMBER	
📅 DATE	
⏱ START / END TIME	
📍 LOCATION	
📇 ADDRESS	
👥 CLIENT	
👥 PARTICIPANTS	

SITE INFORMATION

✨ KNOWN HAUNTING	🚪 ROOM/ LOCATION	📄 DESCRIPTION

SUSPECTED ENTITY INFORMATION

POSSIBLE NAMES	
DATES ALIVE	
KNOWN MOTIVE & STORY	

INVESTIGATION RECORDINGS

TEMPERATURE		SENSOR READING 1	
ATMOSPHERE		SENSOR READING 2	

OBSERVATIONS

EQUIPMENT/ INVESTIGATOR	REPORTS & NOTES

PHOTOS/ SKETCHES

🔍 CASE NUMBER	
📅 DATE	
⏱ START / END TIME	
📍 LOCATION	
📇 ADDRESS	
👥 CLIENT	
👥 PARTICIPANTS	

SITE INFORMATION

✦ KNOWN HAUNTING	🚪 ROOM/ LOCATION	📄 DESCRIPTION

SUSPECTED ENTITY INFORMATION

POSSIBLE NAMES	
DATES ALIVE	
KNOWN MOTIVE & STORY	

INVESTIGATION RECORDINGS

TEMPERATURE		SENSOR READING 1	
ATMOSPHERE		SENSOR READING 2	

OBSERVATIONS

EQUIPMENT/ INVESTIGATOR	REPORTS & NOTES

PHOTOS/ SKETCHES

🔍 CASE NUMBER	
🗓 DATE	
⏱ START / END TIME	
📍 LOCATION	
📇 ADDRESS	
👥 CLIENT	
👥 PARTICIPANTS	

SITE INFORMATION

✨ KNOWN HAUNTING	🚪 ROOM/ LOCATION	📄 DESCRIPTION

SUSPECTED ENTITY INFORMATION

POSSIBLE NAMES	
DATES ALIVE	
KNOWN MOTIVE & STORY	

INVESTIGATION RECORDINGS

TEMPERATURE		SENSOR READING 1	
ATMOSPHERE		SENSOR READING 2	

OBSERVATIONS

⊘ EQUIPMENT/ INVESTIGATOR	📝 REPORTS & NOTES

PHOTOS/ SKETCHES

🔍 CASE NUMBER	
📅 DATE	
🕐 START / END TIME	
📍 LOCATION	
📇 ADDRESS	
👥 CLIENT	
👥 PARTICIPANTS	

SITE INFORMATION

✦ KNOWN HAUNTING	🚪 ROOM/ LOCATION	📄 DESCRIPTION

SUSPECTED ENTITY INFORMATION

POSSIBLE NAMES	
DATES ALIVE	
KNOWN MOTIVE & STORY	

INVESTIGATION RECORDINGS

TEMPERATURE		SENSOR READING 1	
ATMOSPHERE		SENSOR READING 2	

OBSERVATIONS

EQUIPMENT/ INVESTIGATOR	REPORTS & NOTES

PHOTOS/ SKETCHES

🔍 CASE NUMBER	
📅 DATE	
🕐 START / END TIME	
📍 LOCATION	
📇 ADDRESS	
👥 CLIENT	
👥 PARTICIPANTS	

SITE INFORMATION

✨ KNOWN HAUNTING	🚪 ROOM/ LOCATION	📄 DESCRIPTION

SUSPECTED ENTITY INFORMATION

POSSIBLE NAMES	
DATES ALIVE	
KNOWN MOTIVE & STORY	

INVESTIGATION RECORDINGS

TEMPERATURE		SENSOR READING 1	
ATMOSPHERE		SENSOR READING 2	

OBSERVATIONS

EQUIPMENT/ INVESTIGATOR	REPORTS & NOTES

PHOTOS/ SKETCHES

🔍 CASE NUMBER	
📅 DATE	
🕐 START / END TIME	
📍 LOCATION	
📇 ADDRESS	
👥 CLIENT	
👥 PARTICIPANTS	

SITE INFORMATION

✦ KNOWN HAUNTING	🚪 ROOM/ LOCATION	📄 DESCRIPTION

SUSPECTED ENTITY INFORMATION

POSSIBLE NAMES	
DATES ALIVE	
KNOWN MOTIVE & STORY	

INVESTIGATION RECORDINGS

TEMPERATURE		SENSOR READING 1	
ATMOSPHERE		SENSOR READING 2	

OBSERVATIONS

EQUIPMENT/ INVESTIGATOR	REPORTS & NOTES

PHOTOS/ SKETCHES

🔍 CASE NUMBER	
📅 DATE	
🕐 START / END TIME	
📍 LOCATION	
📇 ADDRESS	
👥 CLIENT	
👥 PARTICIPANTS	

SITE INFORMATION

✧ KNOWN HAUNTING	🚪 ROOM/ LOCATION	📄 DESCRIPTION

SUSPECTED ENTITY INFORMATION

POSSIBLE NAMES	
DATES ALIVE	
KNOWN MOTIVE & STORY	

INVESTIGATION RECORDINGS

TEMPERATURE		SENSOR READING 1	
ATMOSPHERE		SENSOR READING 2	

OBSERVATIONS

EQUIPMENT/ INVESTIGATOR	REPORTS & NOTES

PHOTOS/ SKETCHES

🔍 CASE NUMBER	
📅 DATE	
⏱ START / END TIME	
📍 LOCATION	
📇 ADDRESS	
👥 CLIENT	
👥 PARTICIPANTS	

SITE INFORMATION

✨ KNOWN HAUNTING	🚪 ROOM/ LOCATION	📄 DESCRIPTION

SUSPECTED ENTITY INFORMATION

POSSIBLE NAMES	
DATES ALIVE	
KNOWN MOTIVE & STORY	

INVESTIGATION RECORDINGS

TEMPERATURE		SENSOR READING 1	
ATMOSPHERE		SENSOR READING 2	

OBSERVATIONS

EQUIPMENT/ INVESTIGATOR	REPORTS & NOTES

PHOTOS/ SKETCHES

🔍 CASE NUMBER	
📅 DATE	
🕐 START / END TIME	
📍 LOCATION	
📇 ADDRESS	
👥 CLIENT	
👥 PARTICIPANTS	

SITE INFORMATION

✧ KNOWN HAUNTING	🚪 ROOM/ LOCATION	📄 DESCRIPTION

SUSPECTED ENTITY INFORMATION

POSSIBLE NAMES	
DATES ALIVE	
KNOWN MOTIVE & STORY	

INVESTIGATION RECORDINGS

TEMPERATURE		SENSOR READING 1	
ATMOSPHERE		SENSOR READING 2	

OBSERVATIONS

EQUIPMENT/ INVESTIGATOR	REPORTS & NOTES

PHOTOS/ SKETCHES

🔍 CASE NUMBER	
📅 DATE	
🕐 START / END TIME	
🏠 LOCATION	
📇 ADDRESS	
👥 CLIENT	
👥 PARTICIPANTS	

SITE INFORMATION

✧ KNOWN HAUNTING	⬛ ROOM/ LOCATION	📄 DESCRIPTION

SUSPECTED ENTITY INFORMATION

POSSIBLE NAMES	
DATES ALIVE	
KNOWN MOTIVE & STORY	

INVESTIGATION RECORDINGS

TEMPERATURE		SENSOR READING 1	
ATMOSPHERE		SENSOR READING 2	

OBSERVATIONS

EQUIPMENT/ INVESTIGATOR	REPORTS & NOTES

PHOTOS/ SKETCHES

CASE NUMBER

DATE

START / END TIME

LOCATION

ADDRESS

CLIENT

PARTICIPANTS

SITE INFORMATION

✧ KNOWN HAUNTING	▯ ROOM/ LOCATION	🗎 DESCRIPTION

SUSPECTED ENTITY INFORMATION

POSSIBLE NAMES	
DATES ALIVE	
KNOWN MOTIVE & STORY	

INVESTIGATION RECORDINGS

TEMPERATURE		SENSOR READING 1	
ATMOSPHERE		SENSOR READING 2	

OBSERVATIONS

EQUIPMENT/ INVESTIGATOR	REPORTS & NOTES

PHOTOS/ SKETCHES

🔍 CASE NUMBER	
📅 DATE	
⏱ START / END TIME	
📍 LOCATION	
📇 ADDRESS	
👥 CLIENT	
👥 PARTICIPANTS	

SITE INFORMATION

✨ KNOWN HAUNTING	🚪 ROOM/ LOCATION	📄 DESCRIPTION

SUSPECTED ENTITY INFORMATION

POSSIBLE NAMES	
DATES ALIVE	
KNOWN MOTIVE & STORY	

INVESTIGATION RECORDINGS

TEMPERATURE		SENSOR READING 1	
ATMOSPHERE		SENSOR READING 2	

OBSERVATIONS

EQUIPMENT/ INVESTIGATOR	REPORTS & NOTES

PHOTOS/ SKETCHES

🔍 CASE NUMBER	
📅 DATE	
⏱ START / END TIME	
📍 LOCATION	
📇 ADDRESS	
👥 CLIENT	
👥 PARTICIPANTS	

SITE INFORMATION

✨ KNOWN HAUNTING	🚪 ROOM/ LOCATION	📄 DESCRIPTION

SUSPECTED ENTITY INFORMATION

POSSIBLE NAMES	
DATES ALIVE	
KNOWN MOTIVE & STORY	

INVESTIGATION RECORDINGS

TEMPERATURE		SENSOR READING 1	
ATMOSPHERE		SENSOR READING 2	

OBSERVATIONS

EQUIPMENT/ INVESTIGATOR	REPORTS & NOTES

PHOTOS/ SKETCHES

🔍 CASE NUMBER	
📅 DATE	
🕐 START / END TIME	
📍 LOCATION	
📇 ADDRESS	
👥 CLIENT	
👥 PARTICIPANTS	

SITE INFORMATION

✧ KNOWN HAUNTING	🚪 ROOM/ LOCATION	📄 DESCRIPTION

SUSPECTED ENTITY INFORMATION

POSSIBLE NAMES	
DATES ALIVE	
KNOWN MOTIVE & STORY	

INVESTIGATION RECORDINGS

TEMPERATURE		SENSOR READING 1	
ATMOSPHERE		SENSOR READING 2	

OBSERVATIONS

EQUIPMENT/ INVESTIGATOR	REPORTS & NOTES

PHOTOS/ SKETCHES

🔍 CASE NUMBER	
📅 DATE	
🕐 START / END TIME	
📍 LOCATION	
📇 ADDRESS	
👥 CLIENT	
👥 PARTICIPANTS	

SITE INFORMATION

✨ KNOWN HAUNTING	🚪 ROOM/ LOCATION	📄 DESCRIPTION

SUSPECTED ENTITY INFORMATION

POSSIBLE NAMES	
DATES ALIVE	
KNOWN MOTIVE & STORY	

INVESTIGATION RECORDINGS

TEMPERATURE		SENSOR READING 1	
ATMOSPHERE		SENSOR READING 2	

OBSERVATIONS

EQUIPMENT/ INVESTIGATOR	REPORTS & NOTES

PHOTOS/ SKETCHES

CASE NUMBER

🔍 CASE NUMBER	
📅 DATE	
⏱ START / END TIME	
📍 LOCATION	
📇 ADDRESS	
👥 CLIENT	
👥 PARTICIPANTS	

SITE INFORMATION

✧ KNOWN HAUNTING	🚪 ROOM/ LOCATION	📄 DESCRIPTION

SUSPECTED ENTITY INFORMATION

POSSIBLE NAMES	
DATES ALIVE	
KNOWN MOTIVE & STORY	

INVESTIGATION RECORDINGS

TEMPERATURE		SENSOR READING 1	
ATMOSPHERE		SENSOR READING 2	

OBSERVATIONS

EQUIPMENT/ INVESTIGATOR	REPORTS & NOTES

PHOTOS/ SKETCHES

🔍 CASE NUMBER	
📅 DATE	
🕐 START / END TIME	
📍 LOCATION	
📇 ADDRESS	
👥 CLIENT	
👥 PARTICIPANTS	

SITE INFORMATION

✦ KNOWN HAUNTING	🚪 ROOM/ LOCATION	📄 DESCRIPTION

SUSPECTED ENTITY INFORMATION

POSSIBLE NAMES	
DATES ALIVE	
KNOWN MOTIVE & STORY	

INVESTIGATION RECORDINGS

TEMPERATURE		SENSOR READING 1	
ATMOSPHERE		SENSOR READING 2	

OBSERVATIONS

EQUIPMENT/ INVESTIGATOR	REPORTS & NOTES

PHOTOS/ SKETCHES

🔍 CASE NUMBER	
📅 DATE	
🕐 START / END TIME	
📍 LOCATION	
📇 ADDRESS	
👥 CLIENT	
👥 PARTICIPANTS	

SITE INFORMATION

✨ KNOWN HAUNTING	🚪 ROOM/ LOCATION	📄 DESCRIPTION

SUSPECTED ENTITY INFORMATION

POSSIBLE NAMES	
DATES ALIVE	
KNOWN MOTIVE & STORY	

INVESTIGATION RECORDINGS

TEMPERATURE		SENSOR READING 1	
ATMOSPHERE		SENSOR READING 2	

OBSERVATIONS

EQUIPMENT/ INVESTIGATOR	REPORTS & NOTES

PHOTOS/ SKETCHES

Printed in Great Britain
by Amazon

75285994R00066